CONTENTS

Published 2013. Century Books Ltd.
Unit 1, Upside Station Building Solsbro Road,
Torquay, Devon, UK, TQ26FD

books@centurybooksltd.co.uk

centum

Do you ♥ Olly Murs? Yep? Then this brand new 2014 annual will top your reading list. It's the essential guide to all things Olly, 100% official and packed full of facts, photos and fun stuff – happy days! Write your name here so that the world knows that this copy belongs to you.

Name:

_____

_____

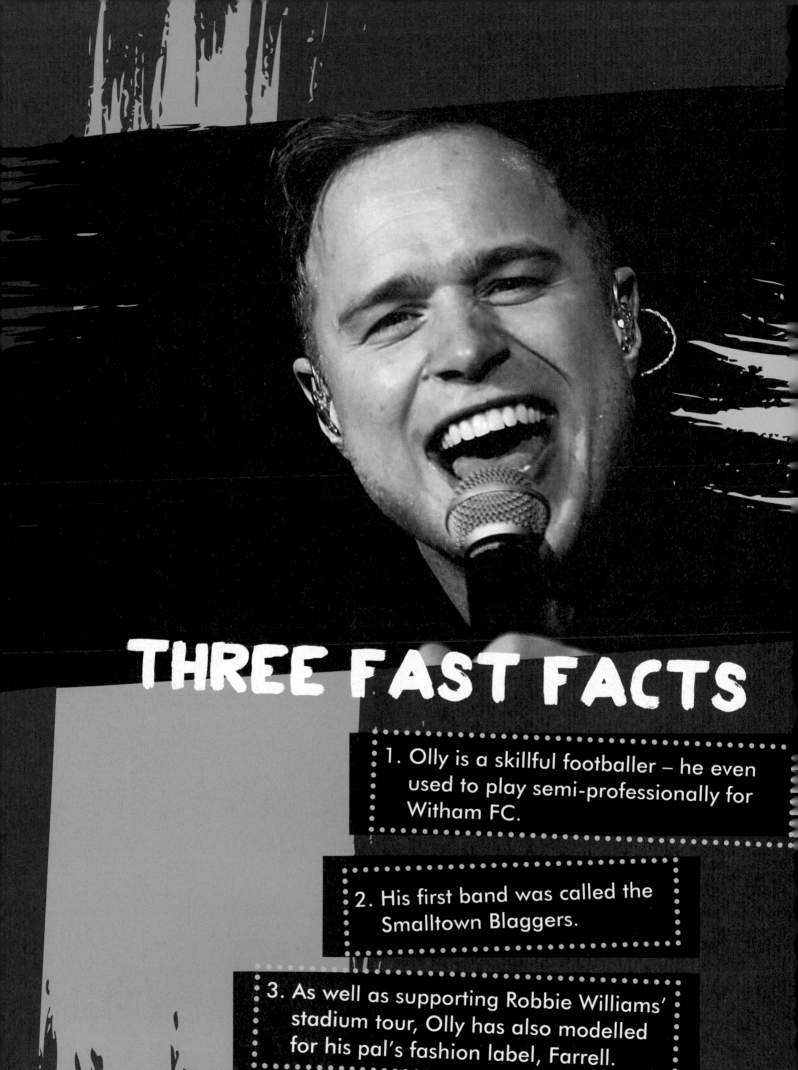

THREE FAST FACTS

1. Olly is a skillful footballer – he even used to play semi-professionally for Witham FC.

2. His first band was called the Smalltown Blaggers.

3. As well as supporting Robbie Williams' stadium tour, Olly has also modelled for his pal's fashion label, Farrell.

IT'S ALL ABOUT OLLY!

HE'S THE ESSEX BOY THAT CAPTIVATED A WHOLE NATION – NOW ALL GROWN UP AND RENOWNED AS A GLOBAL RECORDING ARTIST! OLLY HAS COME A LONG WAY SINCE HE BURST ONTO OUR SCREENS IN 2009. FOUR YEARS DOWN THE LINE, THE STAR HAS THREE HIT ALBUMS, FOUR NUMBER ONE SINGLES AND TWO ARENA TOURS UNDER HIS BELT. AND THAT'S JUST FOR STARTERS ...

Full name ...	Oliver Stanley Murs
Born ...	May 14th, 1984
Star sign ...	Taurus
Home town ...	Witham, Essex
Family ...	Mum, Vicki-Lynn Murs Dad, Peter Murs Sister, Fay Twin brother, Ben
Talents ...	Singing, song-writing, dancing
Big break ...	That performance of *Superstition* for his 2009 *X Factor* audition
Fave footie team ...	Manchester United
Dream holiday destination ...	Barbados
Would be lost without ...	His iPad
Most likely to say ...	*"Oh my days!"*

HAVE YOU SIGNED UP TO THE MURS' ARMY? HERE'S OUR TOP 10 LIST OF REASONS FOR JOINING THE COOLEST FAN FORCE ON THE PLANET ...

1. The dazzling, heart-stopping Olly grin. It's so bright you need to wear shades!

2. His amazing music. Whether it's the vintage beat of *Dance With Me Tonight*, the gotta-dance vibe of *Troublemaker* or the soulful ballad *Dear Darlin'*, Olly's tunes are impossible to resist!

3. His trademark hats and cute skinny jeans.

4. Olly's infectious sense of humour. When Olly's around, you can't help but giggle!

5. His belief in sticking at it and never giving up. Olly's success isn't a coincidence – he's worked for it. Mr Murs is a down-to-earth guy who always puts the time in.

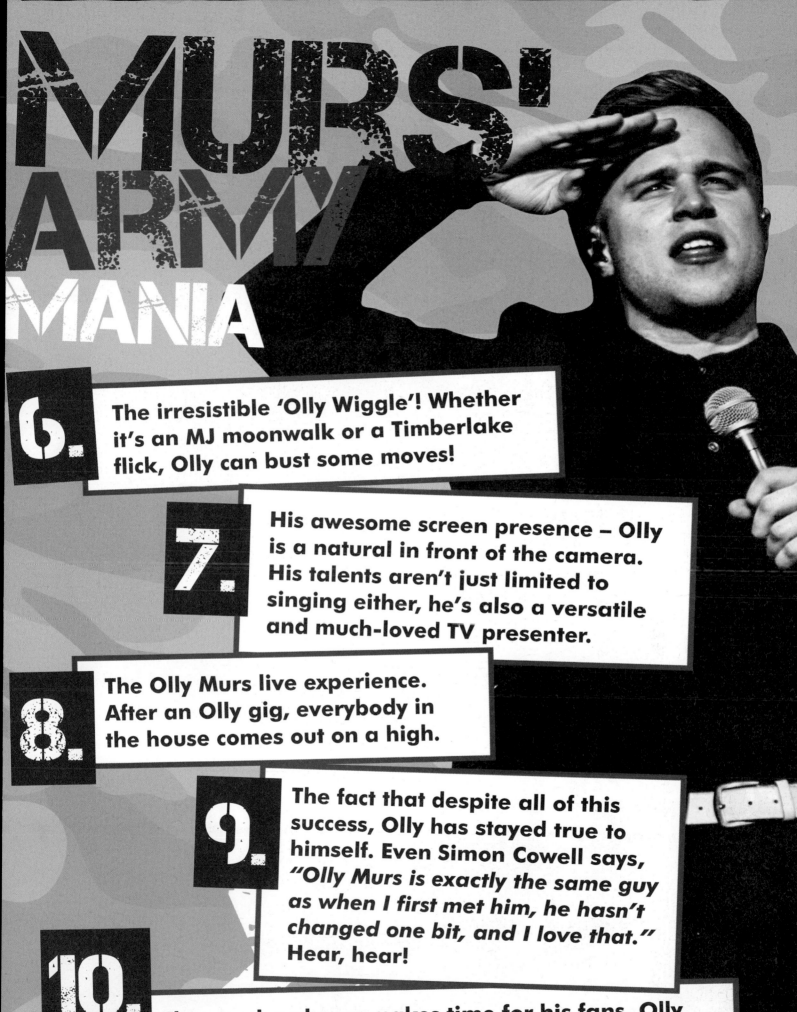

MURS! ARMY MANIA

6. The irresistible 'Olly Wiggle'! Whether it's an MJ moonwalk or a Timberlake flick, Olly can bust some moves!

7. His awesome screen presence – Olly is a natural in front of the camera. His talents aren't just limited to singing either, he's also a versatile and much-loved TV presenter.

8. The Olly Murs live experience. After an Olly gig, everybody in the house comes out on a high.

9. The fact that despite all of this success, Olly has stayed true to himself. Even Simon Cowell says, *"Olly Murs is exactly the same guy as when I first met him, he hasn't changed one bit, and I love that."* Hear, hear!

10. The way he always makes time for his fans. Olly even penned his hit *Army Of Two* to prove just how amazing he thinks you all are!

Born To Perform

When Olly Murs looks back on his performing career, he can hardly believe how far he has come. Now a major face on the music scene, the star has a shelf groaning with awards and multi-platinum records! Everyone knows that Olly's success was kick-started by a brilliant break on national TV, but what they don't know is that his talent was always there, right from the very beginning.

For the Murs family, singing and dancing is in the genes. Olly's great auntie Pat was a professional singer in the West End of London and his nan used to perform in country clubs. Way back in the 1930s his great-great gran was a trapeze artist in the most famous circus in Latvia. No wonder then, that Olly grew up singing!

But back in the early days living with his parents in Witham, Olly only sang for fun. In his mind his career was already mapped out – he was going to be a professional football player. It was only when he got into his early twenties and started to watch *The X Factor* that he dared to dream of something different. For the first time ordinary people like him were getting the chance to try for a career in the music industry! Olly joined the queues and auditioned twice. Twice the producers said, 'No'.

After his failed *The X Factor* auditions, Olly was at an all-time low. He'd seriously injured his knee playing football and although he was now part of a band called the *Smalltown Blaggers*, he felt lost in life. He had reached his mid-twenties without anything to show for it. Olly didn't have a car or a decent job, and he still lived at home with his parents. He made one decision – he would give *The X Factor* one last try. If he couldn't progress this time, that would be it …

The BIG Break

When Olly turned up to audition for *The X Factor* for the third time, he didn't dare get his hopes up. The queues of contestants snaked around the block and everybody who came out seemed to have landed a rejection. This time, however, things were different. A last minute decision to perform Stevie Wonder's *Superstition* left the producers of the show clamouring for more. A couple of weeks later Olly got the callback inviting him to perform on screen for Simon Cowell.

The day that Olly travelled to the ExCel Centre was a life-changer. Inside 2,000 people and four famous judges were ready and waiting to see what he could do, on a show that would be piped to millions of front rooms up and down the country! Olly nervously stepped onto the stage. From the very first note, the atmosphere was electric. The judges raved about him and the audience leapt up for a standing ovation!

Olly was on cloud nine – he'd finally got a sign that he could make it as a performer! The rest of the series was a rollercoaster. After the highs and lows of boot camp and the judges' houses came the pressure of the live finals. It was a nerve-wracking time, but during those live performances Olly found his own blend of retro, white-boy soul. It was old school and the audience loved it!

When the final arrived, only Olly, Stacey Solomon and Joe McElderry were left in the running. After a sensational performance with Robbie, Olly finished in second place to Joe. Olly was gutted. He wasn't to know that despite being pipped to the post, he would go on to become the most successful male artist ever to graduate from *The X Factor*!

"Olly, I've gotta tell you, I really, really like you. And, you know what, you are very, very, very cool ... This is the easiest 'yes' I've ever given!"

Simon Cowell

13

Super Smashing Special

After *The X Factor*, Olly entered a whole new chapter of his life. During the song-writing, albums and concerts that have followed, he has formed a unique connection with his fans and crafted a respected catalogue of brilliant pop hits.

Olly's first single was *'Please Don't Let Me Go'* – a summery, chirpy tune that rocketed straight to number one. He followed it with *'Thinking Of Me'*, his debut album *'Olly Murs'* and a string of hit records. With each new release, Olly's old school ska sound has grown and developed, culminating with the awesome third album *'Right Place Right Time'*.

Along the way, there have been almost too many highlights to count. Olly has toured with One Direction in the USA, presented *The Xtra Factor* with Caroline Flack, sold out his own dazzling headline arena tour and appeared as Robbie Williams' special guest in some of Europe's biggest stadia. Other artists queue up to work, write and perform with him – from hip hop duo Rizzle Kicks to rapping legend Flo Rida.

Who knows where the Olly rollercoaster will take us next? Whether it's the main stage of a summer festival or the set of a stunning new music video, the Murs' Army can't wait to share the ride!

Olly works hard at everything he does, putting his heart and soul into every line of every song. His massive talent and loveable personality have firmly established him as one the most successful male artists of the last decade. The story for 2014 remains to be told, but one thing is for sure — it's going to be a blast!

OLLY MURS

Olly Murs
CROSSWORD

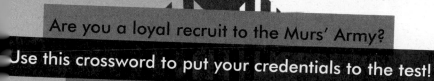

Are you a loyal recruit to the Murs' Army? Use this crossword to put your credentials to the test!

Grab a pen then work your way through the horizontal and vertical crossword clues, writing each answer into the grid.

Will you earn your stripes? Let's see ...

Across

1. Olly's favourite sport.
3. The star's official Twitter feed, @olly_____.
5. The first name of the presenter of *Deal Or No Deal*.
7. The role that Olly plays for the Football Association.
11. The final word of the hit *'Heart Skips A _ _ _ _'*.
12. The surname of the singer who pipped Olly to win *The X Factor*.
14. The place where Olly was born.
15. Olly's old pub band, the *Smalltown _ _ _ _ _ _ _ _*.

Down

1. The rap star that guested on *'Troublemaker'*.
2. The show Olly presented with Caroline Flack.
4. The name of Olly's sister.
6. Olly's star sign.
8. One of Olly's celebrity supporters, _ _ _ _ _ _ _ Bublé.
9. Olly's middle name.
10. The artist Olly toured stadiums with in the summer of 2013.
11. The single release with the shortest title.
13. The surname of Olly's mentor and record boss.

Olly Murs, Rizzle Kicks and a catchy ska melody are the perfect recipe for a summer hit! When *'Heart Skips A Beat'* was released in August 2011 the tune flew straight to number one, eventually selling over 655,000 copies. No one should be surprised – the laidback reggae vibe is classic Olly!

Olly and his pals filmed the video for *'Heart Skips A Beat'* at Mile End Skate Park in East London. It shows Olly dancing, skipping and having a laugh on a giant revolving vinyl record. Look out for the awesome hula-hoop girl, cool skaters, BMX riders and breakdancers all doing their thing to the beat.

So how well do you know Olly's hit? Sing along to the lyrics, filling in the missing words. If you get stuck, you'll find the answers on page 92.

Olly Murs Heart Skips A Beat Feat. Rizzle Kicks

HEART
SKIPS A BEAT

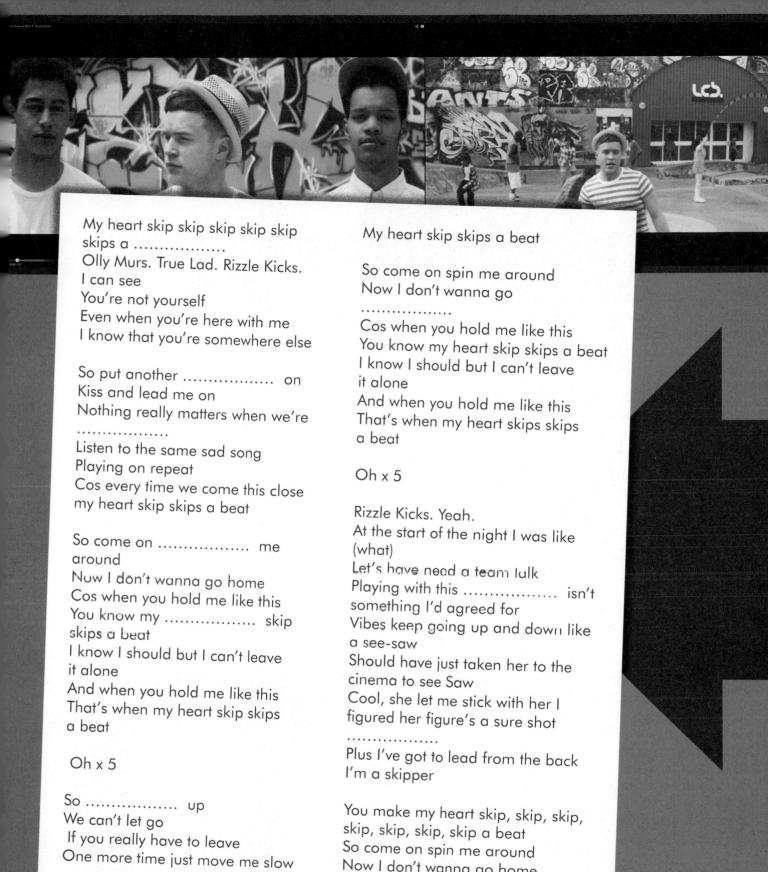

My heart skip skip skip skip skip
skips a ....
Olly Murs. True Lad. Rizzle Kicks.
I can see
You're not yourself
Even when you're here with me
I know that you're somewhere else

So put another .... on
Kiss and lead me on
Nothing really matters when we're
....
Listen to the same sad song
Playing on repeat
Cos every time we come this close
my heart skip skips a beat

So come on .... me
around
Now I don't wanna go home
Cos when you hold me like this
You know my .... skip
skips a beat
I know I should but I can't leave
it alone
And when you hold me like this
That's when my heart skip skips
a beat

Oh x 5

So .... up
We can't let go
If you really have to leave
One more time just move me slow

So put another record on
Play it on ....
Nothing really matters when we're
dancing
Cos all you ever need to know
Is what you do to me
And every time you ....
me close

My heart skip skips a beat

So come on spin me around
Now I don't wanna go
....
Cos when you hold me like this
You know my heart skip skips a beat
I know I should but I can't leave
it alone
And when you hold me like this
That's when my heart skips skips
a beat

Oh x 5

Rizzle Kicks. Yeah.
At the start of the night I was like
(what)
Let's have need a team lulk
Playing with this .... isn't
something I'd agreed for
Vibes keep going up and down like
a see-saw
Should have just taken her to the
cinema to see Saw
Cool, she let me stick with her I
figured her figure's a sure shot
....
Plus I've got to lead from the back
I'm a skipper

You make my heart skip, skip, skip,
skip, skip, skip, skip a beat
So come on spin me around
Now I don't wanna go home
Cos when you hold me like this
You know my heart skips skips a
beat
I know I should but I can't leave it
....
And when you hold me like this
That's when my heart skips skips
a beat

DISCOGRAPHY

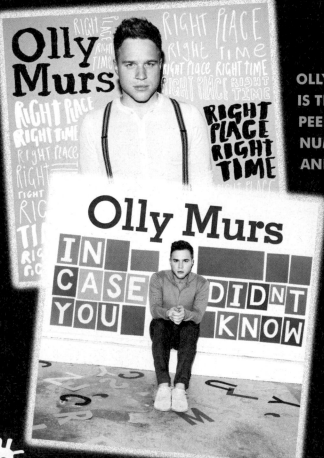

OLLY'S MUSIC CATALOGUE IS THE ENVY OF HIS PEERS. FOUR SMASH HIT NUMBER ONE SINGLES AND THREE DAZZLING ALBUMS HAVE ESTABLISHED HIM AS ONE OF THE UK'S LEADING MALE ARTISTS. HERE'S OLLY'S DISCOGRAPHY IN ALL ITS GLORY – HOW MANY HAVE BEEN PART OF THE SOUNDTRACK OF YOUR WORLD?

THE ALBUMS

Right Place Right Time
Released 23rd November 2012
Charted no.1
Double platinum

In Case You Didn't Know
Released 25th November 2011
Charted no.1
Triple platinum

Olly Murs
Released 26th November 2010
Charted no.2
Double Platinum

THE SINGLES

Dear Darlin'
Released 24th May 2013
Charted no.5

Army Of Two
Released 22nd March 2013
Charted no.12

Troublemaker Feat. Flo Rida
Released 16th November 2012
Charted no.1
Platinum

Oh My Goodness
Released 30th March 2012
Charted no.13

Dance With Me Tonight
Released 18th November 2011
Charted no.1
Platinum

Heart Skips A Beat
Released 21st August 2011
Charted no.1
Platinum

Busy (EP)
Released 27th May 2011
Charted no.45

Heart On My Sleeve
Released 4th March 2011
Charted no.20

Thinking Of Me
Released 19th November 2010
Charted no.4
Gold

Please Don't Let Me Go
Released 27th August 2010
Charted no.1
Gold

23

THE OFFICIAL OLLY QUIZ PART 1

As a passionate footballer and general sports fanatic, it goes without saying that Olly is super-competitive! Is your Olly knowledge poor or prize-winning? The star has decided to set you a challenge to find out! Study the questions, ticking the right answer each time. It's multiple choice madness!

1. Where was the video for 'Dance With Me Tonight' filmed?

a. London ☐
b. Paris ☐
c. Miami, Florida ☐

2. Who has described Olly as "the best risk I've ever taken in my life"?

a. Louis Walsh ☐
b. Robbie Williams ☐
c. Simon Cowell ☐

3. Which class game did O obsessed w 2012 tour?

a. Donkey Kong ☐
b. Sonic the He ☐
c. Pacman ☐

4. How many times Olly has entered *The X Factor*?

a. Three times ☐
b. Twice ☐
c. Four times ☐

5. What is the name of the first track on 'Right Place Right Time'?

a. 'What A Buzz' ☐
b. 'Army Of Two' ☐
c. 'Hand On Heart' ☐

6. Who supported Olly on his 2013 tour?

a. Little Mix ☐
b. Loveable Rogues ☐
c. Rizzle Kicks ☐

7. Where did Olly go for his first holiday after his success in *The X Factor*?

a. Malia ☐
b. Manhattan ☐
c. Madagascar ☐

8. What charity did Olly support when he took part in celebrity *Deal Or No Deal*?

a. Brainwave ☐
b. Barnardo's ☐
c. Battersea Dogs Home ☐

9. What band did when he went o for his 2012 are

a. The Ordinary Boy ☐
b. Madness ☐
c. The Specials ☐

10. What lucky charm did Olly wear all through _The X Factor_?

a. A ring ☐
b. A necklace ☐
c. Beads ☐

11. Where did Olly go to school?

a. Notley High School ☐
b. Basildon Comprehensive ☐
c. Chelmsford Boys ☐

12. What football team does Olly support?

a. Chelsea ☐
b. Manchester City ☐
c. Manchester United ☐

13. In 2011, how did Olly raise money for Comic Relief?

☐
☐
☐

14. What was the first album that Olly ever bought?

a. Kylie _'Fever'_ ☐
b. Meatloaf _'Bat Out Of Hell'_ ☐
c. Michael Jackson _'Thriller'_ ☐

15. Which of Olly's lyric videos did the fans help create?

a. _'Heart Skips A Beat'_ ☐
b. _'Dear Darlin'_ ☐
c. _'Dance With Me Tonight'_ ☐

Olly Murs

RIGHT TIME
RIGHT PLACE
RIGHT TIME
RIGHT PLACE

"This album is the best I've done, so it needs to breathe and for people to hear it."

Olly was thrilled to bits when his third studio album hit the shops — we all loved it just as much as he did! 'Right Place Right Time' revealed how far Olly had come as a musician and performer as well as showcasing his growing gift for song-writing. The disc sold 127,000 copies in its first week on sale, making it the fastest selling album by a male solo artist in the UK charts. When Olly then released 'Troublemaker' as a single, he was lucky enough to score a simultaneous number one in both the single and album charts. He's only the fourth artist to have achieved this, earning a place in the company of Gary Barlow, Robbie Williams and One Direction.

For this album, Olly's sound has evolved a stage further, reflecting some of the music that inspired him during the writing process. The tunes have a funkier feel, reminding Olly of artists such as Jamiroquai and Maroon 5. As well as catchy 'gotta dance' pop tunes, there are heartfelt ballads and stomping anthems too. What's your favourite track?

Olly chose the title 'Right Place Right Time' because it summed up his career to date. He says, "I've worked hard at everything I've done, doing what's felt right, and everything has fitted into place. It's the sentiment for the album — a body of work of great pop songs. And I've gone to a different place again this time."

Right Place Right Time – track listing

- Army Of Two
- Troublemaker' Feat. Flo Rida
- Loud & Clear
- Dear Darlin'
- Right Place Right Time
- Hand On Heart
- Hey You Beautiful
- Head To Toe
- Personal
- What A Buzz
- Cry Your Heart Out
- One Of These Days

CHEEKY CHAP!

As well as having bags of talent, Olly has a unique style that is all of his own. His retro look features key pieces such a penny loafers, blazers and polo shirts. The star also has to take credit for singlehandedly reviving the pork pie hat!

Olly loves to support iconic British brands such as Ben Sherman and Fred Perry, but he shops vintage and high street too. For him it's all about feeling comfortable and believing in yourself – choosing clothes that look good without trying too hard to be someone that you're not. It's a philosophy that works a treat. Whether he's singing into a mic or chatting on the street with his fans, Olly always stands out from the crowd!

THE ESSENTIAL OLLY KIT

What's inside Olly's wardrobe? Take a peek and you'll discover a few key pieces that he wears time and time again.

1. THE TRILBY

2. THE GRANDAD SHIRT

Olly has favoured these from day one. The collarless granddad shirt has an old-fashioned feel that works brilliantly with twisted jeans or chinos.

No one works a hat like Olly! He first started wearing hats during *The X Factor* and hasn't looked back since. As well as being the perfect cure for a bad hair day, Olly's hat fashion gives every outfit the Murs-effect.

3. THE BRACES

Olly often dresses up a shirt and trousers combo by donning a pair of braces. As well as looking sharp, they also work perfectly with those granddad shirts!

4. THE STRIPY TEE

When there's a long, hot summer in the offing, Olly pulls on a retro stripy T-shirt. He chooses his colours carefully — opting for petrol blues, tan and muted reds. They also look great with rolled up sleeves.

5. THE SMART SHOE

Olly is passionate about his footwear — often choosing British design classics such as brogues or Chelsea boots. Good quality shoes can be dressed up or down. Olly wore the ones in the picture to a movie première.

6. THE RAIN MAC

A sharp mac is compulsory for a great British pop star! Olly channels his style hero Paul Weller every time he puts on his tan trench coat.

7. THE TWEED JACKET

If Olly's really in the mood for playing the classic British gentleman, he slips on a tweed jacket. He likes to pick these up in vintage boutiques, bringing the look up-to-date with a pair of jeans. In this shot with Robbie, he's added a waistcoat, too.

8. THE TURNED UP SHORTS

Style is all about picking the right look for the right moment. When the sun comes out, Olly pulls on a pair of turned-up shorts. Whether shop bought or cut down at home, they're an old school staple!

OLLY MURS

A Tee By Me

Fancy having a go as Olly's stylist? Now's your chance! Olly's sporting a clean white tee ready for you to design. Find some pens or pencils and get creative. Will you draw a funky pattern or pepper it with cool graphics – Olly's new look is in your hands!

Telly Talk

Olly performs on the *Wetten, Dass ...?* TV show in Majorca, Spain.

Olly isn't just at the top of his game in the music biz, he's a knockout TV star too! His lovable personality and cheeky Essex patter has made him a sought after guest on the talk show scene. Two years fronting *The Xtra Factor* have also proved that Olly is a brilliant television presenter. He really is the whole package!

Olly had a riot hosting *The Xtra Factor*, but he definitely had to hit the ground running. He says that, *"The first day of filming was in Birmingham. I was lined up to co-present with Caroline Flack; a gorgeous, great presenter and a lovely person. Me and Caz got into a dressing room and I was expecting some training, a little guidance, as I'd never done TV presenting before, but they just left us there to chat for about 20 minutes, then they came in and said, 'Let's go, let's start!'"*

Olly on *Celebrity Juice*

Having a laugh with Caroline Flack at *The Xtra Factor* auditions!

Luckily Olly stayed calm and did a great job. The camera loved him and he was a hit with the audience as well. Olly relished every moment on *The Xtra Factor* and would still be on the show this year if his music commitments didn't take up so much time. Now that's he's moved onto fresh challenges, newcomer Matt Richardson has been recruited to replace him.

In April 2012, Olly got to star in his very own entertainment show. *Life On Murs* followed the artist on his first UK arena tour. As well as offering exclusive behind the scenes access, viewers got to see Olly larking about with his band mates and

After making his name in the UK, Olly was made up to be invited to play a role in the US teen TV series *90210*. Olly got to play himself for his acting début, performing at a birthday party hosted by characters Liam and Navid. Olly has always wanted to act, so appearing on such an iconic show was a dream come true.

Now being tailed by a camera crew has almost become second nature to Olly. Whether he's filming a video diary, sitting on a couch promoting his music or performing one of his songs, Olly's a shining star of the small screen!

MIX IT UP!

Oh my days! Olly's iPod has malfunctioned in spectacular fashion! Can you make head or tail of the jumbled song titles? The track list is made up of brilliant Olly Murs' tunes — find a pen, unscramble the anagrams then write your answers in the spaces underneath.

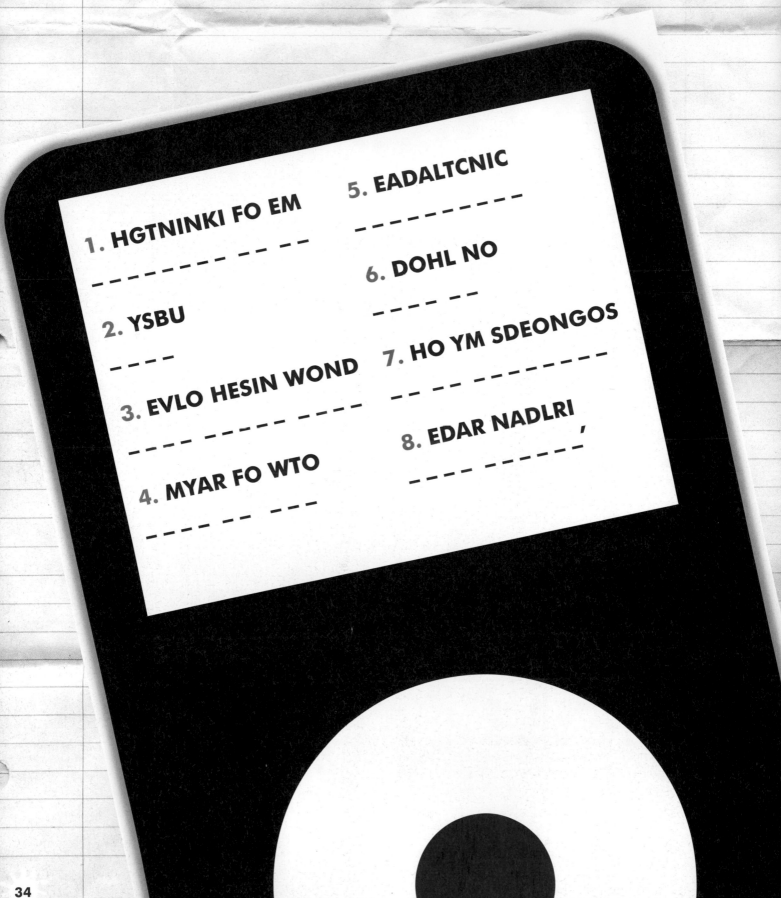

1. HGTNINKI FO EM

_ _ _ _ _ _ _ _ _ _ _ _

2. YSBU

_ _ _ _

3. EVLO HESIN WOND

_ _ _ _ _ _ _ _ _ _ _ _ _

4. MYAR FO WTO

_ _ _ _ _ _ _ _ _ _

5. EADALTCNIC

_ _ _ _ _ _ _ _ _ _

6. DOHL NO

_ _ _ _ _ _

7. HO YM SDEONGOS

_ _ _ _ _ _ _ _ _ _ _ _

8. EDAR NADLRI

_ _ _ _ _ _ _ _ _ _ ,

SONG-WRITING Secrets

As well as being an awesome performer, Olly can boast song-writing credits in all of his albums. As he's grown and developed as an artist, he has got more and more involved in the creative process, honing and shaping his own distinctive sound.

When it comes to sitting in the studio and getting down to the business of writing, inspiration can come from any direction. Some tunes, such as *Please Don't Let Me Go* are based on true events and memories from Olly's own life. Others are influenced by artists that mean a lot to him. *I Need You Now* for example, was inspired by the poignant love songs of Adele.

During the last few years, Olly has worked with some brilliant co-writers from both sides of the Atlantic. When he goes to a writing session with a new collaborator, he tries to get to know the person he's writing with first, so that they both feel relaxed and comfortable working together. This was the case when *Dear Darlin'* was crafted. Olly spent ages chatting to co-writer Ed Drewett, sharing experiences and swapping memories before they put pen to paper. It really helped the pair open up to each other, and pour the emotion Olly wanted into the song.

One of the tunes that Olly is most proud of writing has got to be *Army Of Two*. He explains that, *"I wanted to write a song about my fans who have been amazing to me through the last three years, in the vein of Take That or Coldplay."* The result was a storming pop anthem that captures the spirit of togetherness that Olly and his fans share.

Olly is sure that writing his own songs adds something magical to his performances. By the time he gets to recording in the studio, he knows every one inside out. He doesn't just add vocals, he sings from the heart.

Did you know?

The song Olly wishes that he'd written is Paolo Nutini's *'Pencil Full Of Lead'*.

35

IN CASE YOU

- When Olly performed *Dance With Me Tonight* for the first time on *The X Factor* he sang the song with the cast of *The Muppets!* Animal played drums while Fozzie Bear strummed along the double bass. Diva Miss Piggy even joined in the fun!

- In 2011, Olly did a desert trek in Kenya for Comic Relief. He and a group of other celebrities including Scott Mills and Kara Tointon walked 100 kilometres in blistering 40 degree heat. He described joining the trek as a 'privilege'.

- Olly's all-time fave movie is *The Goonies*.

- Olly absolutely loves his sleep. He'll sleep anywhere and everywhere!

- When he was asked to pose in front of a *'Twitter Mirror'* at the Capital FM's Summertime Ball, Olly treated his fans to a quick chest flash!

DIDN'T KNOW

• Way back in 2007, when Olly appeared on Noel Edmonds' quiz show *Deal Or No Deal*, he left with just £10 in his pocket. He returned for the celebrity edition a few years later, but only managed to win a measly 50p! Maybe it's not your show, Olly!

• Despite not having much luck on 'Deal or No Deal', Olly has also appeared on the quiz show *Who Wants To Be A Millionaire?* He and his mum were part of a charity Mother's Day special episode.

• Once when he performed the tune *On My Cloud* at the Sheffield Arena poor Olly sat down and split his trousers. Awkward! He had the same wardrobe malfunction when he shot a video for Sports Relief.

• Olly is so besotted with his baby nephew Louie, he even has a picture of him on the ear-piece he wears when he performs on stage!

• Olly and his twin brother Ben were born very close together, but Olly can lay claim on being the eldest.

• His favourite sweets are Barrett's Dip Dabs – they're his total weakness!

DANCE WITH ME TONIGHT

POLICE DEPARTMENT
OLLY MURS
20 II 2011 TS
64E2 - W   DIR M·L

When Olly co-wrote *Dance With Me Tonight* he had an axe to grind! The star claimed that he was fed up with Twitter and Facebook dating, preferring to meet new girls in person. Instead of social networking, he wanted to go to a bar and get to know someone properly, just like they used to in the old days.

The song has a classic, Motown feel with a do-wop beat that you can't help tapping your toes to. When it topped the charts in December 2011, there was a whole army of girls queuing up to get to know Olly face-to-face! The video tells the story of Olly being arrested for setting up a street party to woo a mysterious blonde girl called Jamie Winters.

Cue up *Dance With Me Tonight* on your mobile or MP3, then sing along to the words. Can you fill in all the gaps in the lyrics?

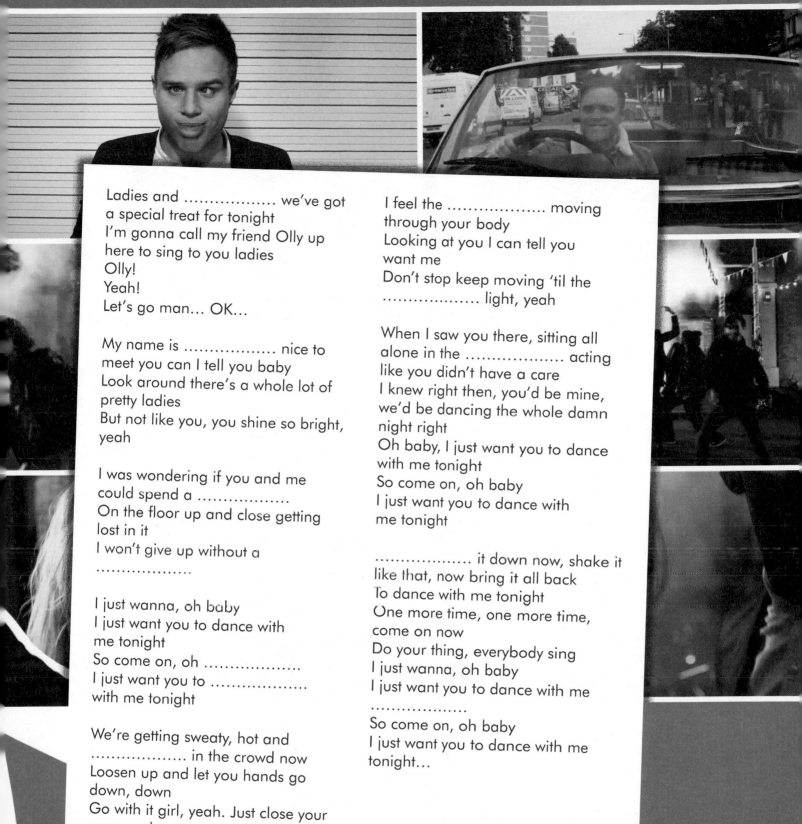

Ladies and .... we've got a special treat for tonight
I'm gonna call my friend Olly up here to sing to you ladies
Olly!
Yeah!
Let's go man... OK...

My name is .... nice to meet you can I tell you baby
Look around there's a whole lot of pretty ladies
But not like you, you shine so bright, yeah

I was wondering if you and me could spend a ....
On the floor up and close getting lost in it
I won't give up without a
....

I just wanna, oh baby
I just want you to dance with me tonight
So come on, oh ....
I just want you to .... with me tonight

We're getting sweaty, hot and .... in the crowd now
Loosen up and let you hands go down, down
Go with it girl, yeah. Just close your eyes, yeah

I feel the .... moving through your body
Looking at you I can tell you want me
Don't stop keep moving 'til the .... light, yeah

When I saw you there, sitting all alone in the .... acting like you didn't have a care
I knew right then, you'd be mine, we'd be dancing the whole damn night right
Oh baby, I just want you to dance with me tonight
So come on, oh baby
I just want you to dance with me tonight

.... it down now, shake it like that, now bring it all back
To dance with me tonight
One more time, one more time, come on now
Do your thing, everybody sing
I just wanna, oh baby
I just want you to dance with me
....
So come on, oh baby
I just want you to dance with me tonight...

Dance

The Olly Wiggle

When it comes to performing in front of an audience, *Dance With Me Tonight* is Olly's all-time favourite song. Wanna know why? Simple. Olly says that it's the tune that is guaranteed to make any crowd get up and boogie! If he can see the audience dancing and having a great time, Olly knows that he's done a good job. *Dance With Me Tonight* has a contagious beat – try playing it and not tapping your toes!

The Murs' Army have always loved Olly's moves – that boy has got rhythm! His reputation for being a wicked dancer goes right back to his very first audition on *The X Factor* live show. Simon, Cheryl, Danni and Louis weren't just impressed by Olly's vocals, they couldn't take their eyes off his feet! Olly popped, wiggled and rocked his way through *Superstitious*, Mesmerising the judges and the crowd. The 'whole package' had arrived, ready to take the world by storm!

Olly is a natural dancer with an amazing stage presence, so it's no wonder that lots of his songs are brilliant to groove along to. Another reason why *Dance With Me Tonight* has a special place in Olly's heart is because it was the first single that he had to learn proper choreography for the video. Olly loved working with professional dancers and picked up the routine in no time – get in there!

So what are the trademark Olly moves? Here's just a flavour of the steps that the star uses to burn up the dance floor ...

Olly won the UK over when he grooved along to *Superstition*. His step-to-step move near the end of the number was soon labelled the 'Olly Wiggle'. It's tricky to pull off, but practice makes perfect – just crouch, kick to the right, kick to the left and then shake those hips. Fresh!

with you!

The booty shake

Olly thrilled fans on his 2013 arena tour by shaking his butt like Beyoncé. He jumped to the side then rippled his tush in homage to the great diva herself. Olly doesn't do the booty shake very often, but when he does it's not for the fainthearted!

The hop

This was a step that Olly perfected for the *Thinking Of Me* video. It sounds easy – just hop from foot to foot in time to the beat. The only difference was, when Olly did it he nailed the steps whilst standing on the top of a concrete bollard! Don't give yourself a hard time though, there was more than a wee bit of camera trickery involved ...

The shoop shoop

It's pretty tricky to spin one of Olly's old school tunes without working in a shoop shoop or two! All you've got to do is click the fingers on both hands while you step to the right, then repeat it to the left. Got it? Congratulations, you're doing the shoop shoop!

When there's a riff in the melody, Olly does what comes naturally – he freestyles! Whether it's moonwalking, jerking or old-time rock n' roll, he isn't afraid to mix it up and give anything a go! Can you freestyle, Murs-stylee? It's all about feeling the music then letting your feet take control.

Freestyle Murs

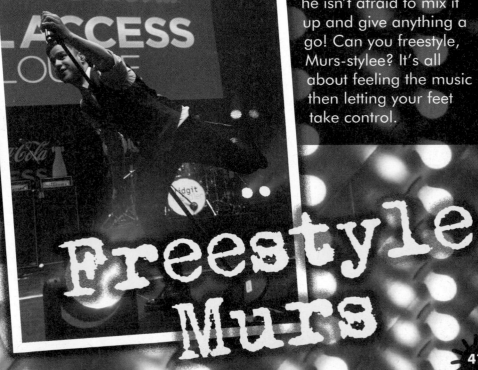

OFF THE RECORD

It doesn't take an exotic location and expensive photo shoot for Olly to shine — he always looks a million dollars! Whether he's been papped, snapped or simply tapped on the shoulder, he always flashes the trademark Murs smile. Here are some pics of our favourite boy caught on camera.

Thumbs up for a signing of 'Right Place Right Time!'

Just catching up on a little retail therapy ...

Time for a quick selfie with fans in Australia

Just Olly, a guitar and a cheeky grin!

Everybody say ch-eeese!

Hats off to Mr Murs!

Stepping out in NYC.

Out and about doing promo in London

Olly is passionate about sport. As a lad he always made the football team, developing such a talent he went on to play semi-professionally for his local side. In fact, if it wasn't for a nasty knee injury, things might have turned out very differently for the star. It was Olly's dream to play in the Premier League, running out on a Saturday for Manchester United. Luckily for us, Olly's plans took a different turn, but football is still a big part of his life.

Being famous has brought Olly lots of opportunities to get involved in the beautiful game. He's appeared on *talkSPORT* radio show and released a DVD called *The Seven Deadly Sins Of Football*! He's even played twice for the England XI Soccer Aid team. Olly can still remember the day that organiser Robbie Williams called him up. *"While I was waiting to release my first single in August 2010, I got a phone call from Robbie Williams ... He said, "Olly, I'm doing this big charity football game again. It's called Soccer Aid, it's a huge event, we will play at either Old Trafford or Wembley in front of 75,000, There'll be loads of celebrities ... looks like we'll have Giggs and Zidane playing. Are you interested?"*

Funnily enough, Olly said a very quick "yes"! Both matches were amazing. Olly got to play next to a host of stars and footballing legends, wearing his England shirt with pride. The games also raised a huge amount of money for UNICEF, with the home side triumphing against the 'Rest of the World'.

In January 2013, Olly was honoured to be appointed as an ambassador for the Football Association. On 6th June 2013, Olly took on his first ever official task. The star went behind-the-scenes at Wembley Stadium, just hours before the England game against the Republic of Ireland! As well as exploring the team's dressing rooms and facilities, Olly got to interview England's kit-men. He even got to print a shirt for Wayne Rooney!

Despite all these honours and privileges, Olly is unflinchingly loyal to the lads in his old team, Notley FC. He sponsors their shirts and even goes back home to play whenever he can. Back of the net!

F⚽OTBALL
Fantastic

Lighting up the *iTunes festival.*

Having a blast in Belfast.

Thrilling the crowds in Times Square, New York.

Working the crowd at the *V Festival*.

46

Giving it everything at the *Fantabuloso Tour* 2013, Chicago Illinois.

Olly is a hugely gifted pop star and presenter, but when he picks up a microphone his star goes into orbit! He describes singing live as the biggest buzz ever, saying, *"There's no better feeling. It is the best part of the job, the pinnacle for me."*

If you've got tickets to see Olly, brace yourself – whether you're going to a festival, TV studio or a city stadium, you're in for one heck of a show! Here are some pix of our favourite guy in action. Can you feel the electricity crackling off the page?

MURS ON THE MIC

Shaking a leg *T4* on the Beach.

THE RIGHT PLACE RIGHT TIME TOUR

In February 2013, Olly kicked off his first ever arena tour with a sell-out night at the Metro Radio Arena in Newcastle. The *Right Place Right Time* tour was, quite simply, the biggest and most ambitious thing he had ever done.

In the lead-up to the concerts, Olly worked and rehearsed tirelessly with his band. The prospect of headlining at venues the size of Wembley Arena made him more nervous and excited than he'd ever been. As well as learning new dance steps and staging, Olly had to build up his voice so that his vocals would sustain the punishing schedule ahead. The star compares it to training for a marathon. The voice is a muscle after all, and it needed to be built up slowly to cope with singing 21 tracks night after night.

Luckily Olly had a great team around him, plus the determination to put in 110%. When he stepped out on stage the first night, Olly Murs dazzled! He opened with *Army Of Two*, the fans' song – a massive number that got everybody in the party mood. Hit after hit followed, with Olly dancing, crooning and at times even playing piano and acoustic guitar on stage.

The audiences went wild, loving his showmanship and charisma. Olly now says that he had to pinch himself at the end of each night, barely able to believe how brilliantly everything had gone! Olly had proved that he was a true star.

THE SET LIST

ACT ONE
Army Of Two
Dance With Me Tonight
Personal
Thinking Of Me
I've Tried Everything
I Need You Now

ACT TWO
Hey You Beautiful
I'm OK
Hand On Heart
Loud & Clear
Busy
Heart On My Sleeve
Should I Stay or Should I Go/
A Town Called Malice

ACT THREE
Please Don't Let Me Go
Dear Darlin'
One Of These Days
Oh My Goodness
Heart Skips a Beat

ENCORE
Right Place Right Time
Troublemaker

50

ON THE ROAD WITH Robbie

In winter of 2012, Olly received a tantalising offer. His friend Robbie Williams invited him to take part in his massive *Take The Crown* Stadium tour! Together the pair would be travelling all over Europe playing monster venues, including a four-night run at Wembley Stadium! Needless to say, Olly didn't need asking twice!

The tour kicked off in Ireland at the Aviva Stadium. Robbie suggested that Olly joined him onstage for the song *Kids*, a hit he'd originally recorded with Kylie. It was an inspired choice – the performance went down a storm! Robbie described it as one of his favourite moments in the show.

LIVE @ A Venue Near You ...

Olly's tours sell out and festival crowds roar when he's topping the bill. Where will the star perform in 2014? Design a poster advertising a brand new Olly Murs concert in your home town. Is he playing at the local theatre, park or in your front room?

Get arty for Olly!

Social Olly

Olly likes to stay connected to his fans 24/7. Whether it's via Twitter, Facebook or Instagram, he's always got something to share! It's no surprise then that his ever-growing Twitter following has surpassed the 4 million mark! Check out some of Olly's most recent Tweets, then click on to @ollyofficial and follow him, too. You never know – if you're lucky he might follow you back!

'OH MY DAYS!! Just landed in ROME... Sch-wing, Sch-wing ... SHAAAAAA-WING!!'

'Drank Red Bull all day yesterday to keep me awake. Swear it didn't kick it 'til I was in bed last night!!'

'I need the old barnet cut massively!!'

'Horrible feeling when you're on your way to work and you see someone leaving the bar going to bed!! That's when you know it's early!!'

'I ripped and I tripped tonight in Cardiff!! Hilarious!!'

'Just watching *Dinner Date*. These lads can cook. I'm such a terrible cook. This lady would get beans on toast from me with cheese. Haha.'

'Just got to Disneyland!! No matter how old you are Still such a great place to come. Can't wait to bring my nephew here when he's older!!'

'Great afternoon in SWEDEN!! This place is insane ... I need to come over here one weekend and PARTY.'

'Ohhh yesss landed back in UK. Looks like I'm in the south of France! Loving this weather. Ray-Bans on, shorts on, Bit of *UB40* & beer later!'

'It's all fun 'n' games!!'

'I've had a right touch. Gig I'm doing in Germany today is on a theme park ... Awesome!!'

'Good luck to anyone sitting exams today peeps!! Tough time I know ... But just Keep revising & keep calm!! Your journey has only just begun.'

'The sun is shining, the weather is sweet yeah #LegsOut'

'Finally got to bed after an eventful, fun, wet family day at the house! Awesome times! No cuts & bruises just smiles & laughter!! X'

'I'm up & hitting the gym!!! Yesssss I'm shocked myself. ... But it's time to get back fit!!!'

'Yessss hugely gutted I'm not doing @XtraFactor this year. Me & Caz had such a wicked time together. Just wanna focus on music this year!!'

'I do love a good sleep ... If the Olympics did this as a sport I'd be the king dinger-ling!! #goldmedal'

THE OFFICIAL OLLY QUIZ

PART 2

So you're up for round two of Olly's triv challenge? Happy days! This round is a fill-in-the-blanks quiz. Some questions should be a cinch, but others are sure to bamboozle even the greatest fan. All you've got to do is look at the words on the opposite page, then write them into the correct sentences.

1. Olly kicked off his 2013 arena tour with a performance at the Metro Radio Arena in _ _ _ _ _ _ _ _ _.

2. Olly's celebrity pal, _ _ _ _ _ _ _ _' _ _ _ _ _ describes him as a 'like a little brother'.

3. Olly was narrowly beaten by _ _ _ _ _ _ _ _ _ _ _ _ to win the first prize in *The X Factor* 2009.

4. Olly's mum is called _ _ _ _ _ - _ _ _ _ _ _ _ _ _ _.

5. Olly was super proud was his sister gave birth to his first nephew, _ _ _ _ _.

6. The video for *Troublemaker* was shot in _ _ _ _ _ _ _ _ _.

7. For the US release of *Heart Skips A Beat*, Olly was joined by the artist _ _ _ _ _ _ _ _ _.

8. Olly has appeared more than once on *Celebrity Juice* alongside comedian _ _ _ _ _ _ _ _ _ _.

9. Olly first got to know artist _ _ _ _ _ _ _ _ _ _ _ _ _ _, when they duetted *Angels* on The X Factor.

10. When Olly appeared on *The Graham Norton show*, the host made him blush in front of fellow guest, _ _ _ _ _ _ _ _ _.

11. In July 2013, Olly headlined a special gig at the theme park, _ _ _ _ _ _ _ _ _ _ _.

12. When Olly went to visit _ _ _ _ _ _ _ _ _ _ _ in the US, he performed a special acoustic version of *Troublemaker*.

13. Olly is flattered to have made a fan and a friend out of the Canadian superstar, _ _ _ _ _ _ _ _ _ _ _ _.

14. Olly's favourite holiday destination is _ _ _ _ _ _ _ _ _.

15. The artist was thrilled to perform onstage at the *Prince's Trust* concert with Take That star _ _ _ _ _ _ _ _ _ _.

Words to use

BARBADOS
MICHAEL BUBLÉ
KEITH LEMON
MILA KUNIS
GARY BARLOW

DERMOT O'LEARY
LOS ANGELES
VICKI-LYNN POLLARD
LOUIE
NEWCASTLE

JOE MCELDERRY
CHIDDY BANG
ROBBIE WILLIAMS
PEREZ HILTON
ALTON TOWERS

TROUBLE MAKER

Flo Rida:
You're a troublemaker, you're a troublemaker
You ain't nothing but a troublemaker girl.

You had me .... again from the minute you sat down
The way you bite your ....
got my head spinnin' around
After a drink or two I was putty in your hands
I don't know if I have the strength to stand

Oh oh oh
Trouble troublemaker yeah that's your .... name
Oh oh oh
I know you're no good but you're stuck in my brain
And I wanna know

Why does it feel so .... but hurt so bad
My mind keeps saying run as fast as you can
I say I'm done but then you pull me back
I swear you're giving me a .... attack
Troublemaker

It's like you're always there in the corners of my mind
I see a silhouette every time I close my eyes
There must be .... in those fingertips of yours
Cos I keep comin' back again for more

Oh oh oh
Trouble troublemaker yeah that's your middle name
Oh oh oh
I know you're no good but you're stuck in my ....
And I wanna know

Why does it feel so good but hurt so bad
My mind keeps saying .... as fast as you can
I say I'm done but then you pull me back
I swear you're giving me a heart attack
Troublemaker
Why does it feel so good but hurt so bad
My mind keeps saying run as fast as you can
I say I'm done but then you pull me ....
I swear you're giving me a heart attack
Troublemaker

Flo Rida:
Hey now maybe I'm ....
Cos I keep doing the same damn thing
Thinking one day we gonna change
But you know just how to work that back
And make me forget my name
What the hell you do I won't remember
I'll be gone until ....
And you'll show up again next summer
Yeah typical middle name is Prada
Fit you like a glove girl I'm sick of the drama
You're a troublemaker
But damn girl I love the trouble
And can't even explain why

Why does it feel so good but hurt so bad
My mind keeps saying run as fast as you can
I say I'm done but then you pull me back
I swear you're giving me a heart attack
Why does it feel so good but hurt so bad
My mind keeps saying run as fast as you can
I say I'm done but then you pull me back
I swear you're giving me a heart attack
Troublemaker

Troublemaker was the lead single from Olly's third album *Right Place Right Time* – a catchy pop anthem with 'hit' written all over it! When the song hit the top spot for the second week in 2012, Olly achieved the rare feat of topping the album and singles chart simultaneously. No wonder he chose it as the closing tune for his 2013 arena tour! The smash also includes a brilliant cameo by Flo Rida.

Most of the *Troublemaker* video was filmed on location in Los Angeles, but Flo Rida filmed his segment separately from Miami. The video features a klutzy girl that keeps on getting sacked from jobs and bumping into Olly along the way. Lucky lady!

Do you know *Troublemaker* off by heart? Let's find out! Sing the lyrics filling in the missing words along the way.

Hearsay *and*

Journalists love writing news stories about Olly, but sometimes it can be difficult to separate the fact from the fiction. We've poured through the column inches and pulled out some true Mr Murs headlines. Unfortunately we've also slipped a few false, made-up ones in there, too!

Read each of the headlines, then decide whether it's true or false. When you've finished, turn to page 92 to sort the fact from the fiction.

1

OLLY MURS OFFERS BABYSITTING SERVICES TO ROBBIE!

TRUE ☐ FALSE ☐

2

GOOD OLLY!
MURS ADMITS TO GARGLING ICED TEA BEFORE EVERY SHOW

TRUE ☐ FALSE ☐

3

OLLY MURS WANTS TO BE AN ACTION MOVIE TROUBLEMAKER

TRUE ☐ FALSE ☐

4

OLLY MURS ABANDONED CAR TO TAKE TUBE TO BRIT AWARDS

TRUE ☐ FALSE ☐

HEADLINES

5 **MURS ATTACKS!**
POP BOY OLLY IS ALL FIRED UP ACROSS THE POND

TRUE ☐   FALSE ☐

6 **MURS HURT IN ICE CRASH**

TRUE ☐   FALSE ☐

7 **NO MURS-Y! OLLY REFUSES TO SIGN AUTOGRAPHS**

TRUE ☐   FALSE ☐

8 **OILY MURS!**
X-FACTOR HEART-THROB OLLY SHOWS OFF A VERY SPOTTY FACE AND CROSS EYES.

TRUE ☐   FALSE ☐

9 **OH MY DAYS!**
MURS GETS A NEW MUTT

TRUE ☐   FALSE ☐

10 **OLLY MURS ADMITS THAT HE'S A TOURING ADDICT!**

TRUE ☐   FALSE ☐

Olly gets invited to loads of celebrity bashes, premières and awards ceremonies, so he's always under pressure to look his best. For a guy, this can be difficult – he needs to stand out without feeling buttoned up and uncomfortable. Olly always obeys a few simple style rules. For Mr Murs it's all about sharp tailoring, good shoes and playful retro details. Watch and learn boys ...

SHAKEN NOT STIRRED

Sometimes only a tux will do! Olly played it classy for Marvin Humes and Rochelle Wiseman's wedding in July 2012, arriving in stylish black tie.

STREET-SMART

Olly looked every inch the star on stage for his *Right Place Right Time* arena tour. Here he is in March 2013 at Manchester Arena, jujjing up a sharp black suit with white accessories.

BRILLIANT IN BURGUNDY

For the **2011 Cosmopolitan Ultimate Women of the Year Awards**, Olly expertly teamed a burgundy suit with a matching turtleneck. The result? A cool take on sixties' pop fashion.

in the Spotlight

ROCKING THE CAPITAL
Olly wore a perfectly cut three piece suit to the *Capital Rocks* event in November 2012. The combo was set off brilliantly with a pair of double-buckled shoes. Good work!

KEEPIN' IT CASUAL
The Muppets première called for less formal attire than the traditional suited and booted look. Olly hit the right note when he teamed a smart suit jacket with jeans and crêpe shoes, all in muted shades of grey.

I SAY, I SAY!
Not many guys can pull off a cravat, but Mr Murs can! Olly looked devilishly handsome when he arrived at the première for *The A-Team* movie in November 2010.

WOWING IN A WAISTCOAT
Olly owned the red carpet at the **2013 Brit Awards** when he stepped out in a silky double-breasted waistcoat and button-down shirt. Perfect attire for a Best British Male nominee!

DARING IN CHECKS
Olly and his *The Xtra Factor* co-host Caroline Flack made a splash when they arrived at the Pride of Britain Awards. Olly shook things up with a bold check suit and white shirt.

MURS' MEGA WORDSEARCH

O	L	J	E	V	A	R	E	N	A	P	G	M	A
L	W	A	Q	R	R	L	O	A	F	E	R	S	L
L	I	X	D	H	Y	P	P	A	H	X	Z	L	B
Y	T	F	S	O	V	F	M	A	T	E	S	S	U
O	H	L	E	S	M	A	N	A	G	E	R	H	M
F	A	T	U	O	S	D	J	Y	D	V	W	U	N
F	M	I	K	C	N	Q	N	B	C	X	F	O	K
I	T	Y	Z	C	T	M	K	L	Y	K	R	E	E
C	C	H	E	E	K	Y	U	I	M	U	Y	D	C
I	Q	J	L	R	H	H	B	R	O	Z	N	I	N
A	Z	E	W	A	G	A	C	T	S	P	I	V	A
L	L	B	G	I	G	T	M	Y	P	F	W	L	D
S	K	A	P	D	V	F	B	R	N	S	T	I	J
L	A	S	R	A	E	H	E	R	G	D	N	A	B

64

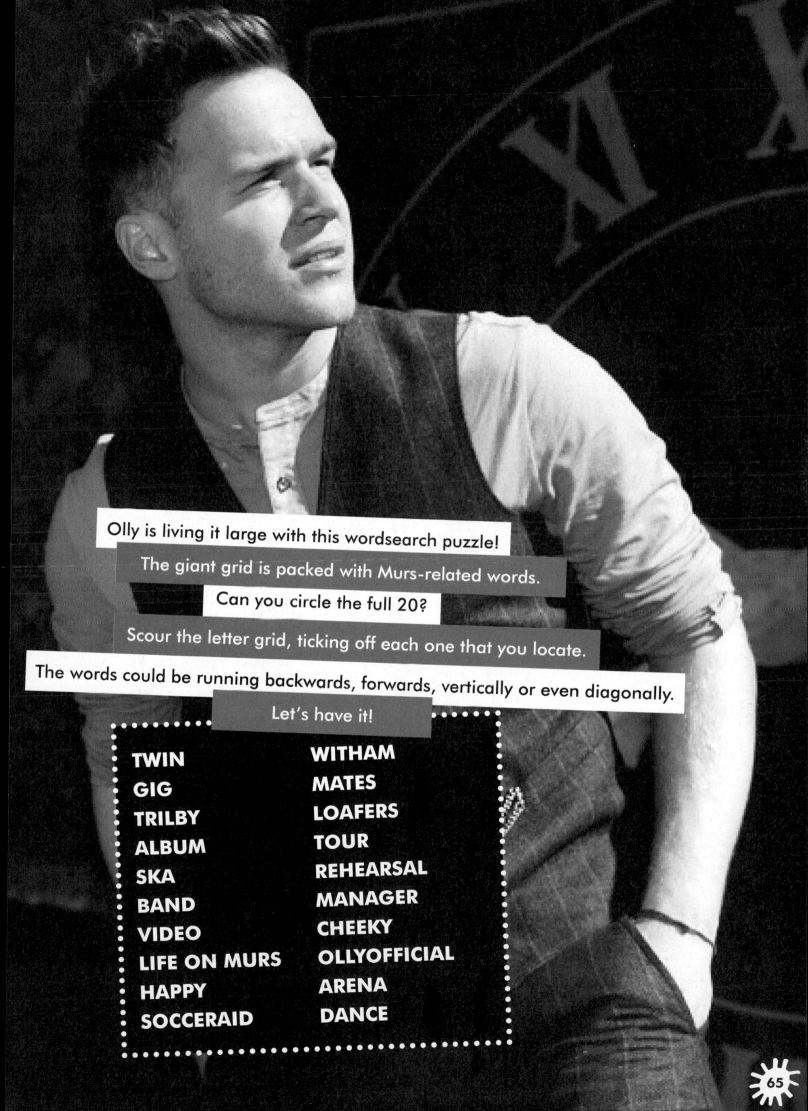

Olly is living it large with this wordsearch puzzle!

The giant grid is packed with Murs-related words.

Can you circle the full 20?

Scour the letter grid, ticking off each one that you locate.

The words could be running backwards, forwards, vertically or even diagonally.

Let's have it!

TWIN	WITHAM
GIG	MATES
TRILBY	LOAFERS
ALBUM	TOUR
SKA	REHEARSAL
BAND	MANAGER
VIDEO	CHEEKY
LIFE ON MURS	OLLYOFFICIAL
HAPPY	ARENA
SOCCERAID	DANCE

"To sell out my first arena tour. It's incredible. It's going to be a really proud moment for the Murs family ... it makes me really emotional actually, thinking about it ... The Murs massive will be in!"
(Olly on the afternoon before his first appearance headlining at the O2 Arena.)

"People relate to me, and I try to make songs to make people smile."

"She can be ruthless at times, she gets me in check, but I need that. I don't think I'd be where I am now if it wasn't for Sarah being in my corner."
(Olly on his manager, Sarah)

"I would have taken an egg for Simon [Cowell] for sure. I would have taken a bullet."
(Olly on the egg-throwing incident at the final of Britain's Got Talent.)

"I think every member of my band brings something different ... they bring out the best in me."
(Olly on his fellow musicians)

"In my eyes I think people are a bit shocked by the song. I'm not because I've always wanted to do a song like that. I think I'm always trying to do something people wouldn't expect."
(Olly on a change of direction with Dear Darlin')

"I wanted to write a song about my fans that have been amazing to me over the last three years ... It felt amazing writing this song and I can't wait to sing it live!"
(Olly on penning Army Of Two)

"They were screaming and shouting my name wherever I went and the situation got completely out of hand."
(Olly describing his first lads holiday after finishing The X Factor)

OLLY
IN HIS OWN

"All I see is flashing lights ... click, click, click ... cameras and phones ... that just gets you even more excited."
(Olly on stepping out on stage at a gig)

"I cherish every single moment that I'm up there, knowing that someday it might not be there anymore. I pretty much perform every gig like it's my last."
(Olly on performing in his arena tour.)

"She was my very first crush. I used to carry pictures of her around with me everywhere. She is gorgeous and still my ideal date."
(Olly on Victoria Beckham)

WORDS

Olly's tour manager, Mark

Whenever Olly is on the road, he knows that his tour manager Mark will be right beside him. The pair have become very close. Olly puts it best when he says, "Mark is my right brain, 'cause he's always on this side of me. He's my best friend. He's my wife! He gets me when I'm cranky, he sees me when I'm happy and when I'm sad. We're with each other every day, 24/7. Mark really sacrifices a lot to be with me and it means a lot. In my eyes he's the best."

FAB FRIENDS

Being such a fun-to-knover guy, it's no wonder that Olly's address book is bursting with celebrity deets! During his time in the limelight the star has built up some strong and lasting friendships. As well as being devoted to his touring band and his manager Sarah, there are some other VIPs that mean the world to Olly ...

Niall Horan

One Direction's crazy-haired Niall is a great mate, who's always up for a giggle. As well as tweeting pictures of each other's chest hair, the pair are regularly spotted socialising. When Olly went on tour with the band in 2012 Niall even joined him behind the scenes to perform an acoustic version of *Heart Skips A Beat*.

JLS

Olly often talks about his friendship with JLS – Oritsé, Marvin, JB and Aston. He's even tweeted 'The @JLSOfficial boys have always been there for me since day one. For support, advice!! Never be forgotten that. See you lads soon!' That friendship was put to the test recently however when the band pranked Olly whilst filming a TV show. Olly was tricked into thinking that he had fired Aston out of a cannon, leaving him hurt or worse! Luckily Olly saw the funny side after he'd found out that his mate was OK. LOL!

Robbie Williams

As far as famous friends go, no one gets more high profile than Robbie Williams! Sometimes Olly can't believe that they are hanging out together! The pair have tons in common – as well as being showmen on stage, they love their football and having a joke with their mates.

Rizzle Kicks

Olly first got to know Jordan and Harley from Rizzle Kicks when they featured on his single *Heart Skips A Beat*. The star hit it off with the Brighton hip hop duo straight away, with Jordan describing Olly as a 'genuinely wicked guy'. The pals share a love of footie and of course, music. Olly has even hinted that he might record another collaboration with the Kicks in the future!

Caroline Flack

Olly and Caroline famously spent two years working together as co-presenters on *The Xtra Factor*. They got incredibly close, but despite all those dating rumours they really are just good friends! The pair had a nice reunion in May 2013 when they partied the night away together at Dermot O'Leary's 40th birthday bash.

Michael Bublé

Canadian megastar Michael Bublé has been hugely supportive of Olly. Michael was impressed with Olly's talent when their paths crossed on *The X Factor*, and he has followed his career with interest. Olly describes Michael as "genuinely one of the nicest guys you will ever meet, and despite his massive success he is still so down-to-earth and, best of all, he doesn't take himself too seriously."

Army Of Two has a very special place in Olly's heart – it's the tune he recorded as a tribute to us, his fans! The star chose to celebrate the Murs' Army with a thumping pop anthem inspired by artists like *Take That* and *Maroon 5*.

The video for the single was released on Valentine's Day, 2013. The footage shows Olly in a deserted car park, walking towards the camera. As he steps forward, the star is gradually joined by more and more identical clones of Olly, all singing along in unison. Before the song is out, a whole army of Ollys are marching towards the future raising their right hands!

Test your army credentials by casting your eye through these lyrics. Use a pen or pencil to fill in all the missing words.

I came, I saw, tore down, those
....
Block one way, I'll find another
You know you'll always be
discovered
If it's me, you choose, I can't lose
I'm in .... with you, if you
love me too, yeah

Don't ever change, and I'll stay
the same
We'll be .... in the same
direction
And we'll never lose this
....
Nothing they can do, can stop this
army of two
We're marching to the future, yeah
it's me and you

So just follow my lead, repeat
after me
Faith is the ....,
hope is the gun
And love is all we need
Now fear's on the run
We've already won
So march with the ....,
raise your right hand
And we've only just begun

I took a vow, to never let you down
When it's us, there ain't no
competition
I can be the star, on which you're
wishing
I never doubted for a ....
it's true
I love all of you, if you love me too,
yeah
Don't ever change, and I'll stay
the same
We'll be swimming in the
same direction
And we'll never lose this connection
Nothing they can do, can stop this

army of two
We're marching to the
.................., just me and you

So just follow my lead, repeat
after me
Faith is the bullet, ...
is the gun
And love is all we need
Now fear's on the run
We've already won
So march with the band, raise your
right hand
And we've only just begun

Only just begun, only just begun

Don't ever ...., and I'll
stay the same
We'll be swimming in the same
direction
And we'll never lose this connection
Nothing they can do, can stop this
army of two
Cos we're marching to the future,
yeah it's me and you

So just follow my lead, repeat
after me
Faith is the bullet, hope is the gun
And love is all we need
Now fear's on the run
We've already won
So march with the band, raise your
right ....
And we've only just begun

It's the moment of truth, I'm
counting on you
This army of two have only
just begun
It's the moment of ....,
I'm counting on you
This army of two have only
just begun

ARMY = ME + YOU!

My date with Olly would begin at ....
....
....

We would start by going to ....
....
....

For lunch we would head to ....
....

The perfect menu would be ....
....

OF TWO

ARE YOU A LOYAL RECRUIT TO TEAM MURS? IF SO, ARMY OF TWO IS DEDICATED TO YOU! WHAT WOULD YOU DO IF YOU HAD OLLY ALL TO YOURSELF ONE DAY? CLOSE YOUR EYES AND TRY TO IMAGINE YOUR PERFECT DATE. WOULD YOU GO SHOPPING, DANCING OR OUT FOR A BITE TO EAT? USE THESE PAGES TO PLAN EVERY DREAMY DETAIL!

In the afternoon we would make a beeline for...................................
....
....

I would like to introduce Olly to ....
....

The music we would listen to would be ....
....

The things we would laugh about would be ....
....

Olly and I would wrap up our perfect date by ....
....

1. "I have worked with him since the day he left *The X Factor*. He's brilliant to work with. He's very, very rarely in a bad mood because he just genuinely loves what he does. He knows what he wants and he's willing to work really hard for it."

(......................... on dealing with Olly the pop star)

2. "He splits his trousers a lot ... his wardrobe department, bless them! He's got rows of trousers lined up, all the same, just in case."

(......................... on Olly Murs' tight trousers)

3. "I've often caught him as I opened the door, in his pants, singing into the remote control." (......................... on how Olly's singing ambitions started at a young age)

4. "There was nothing pretentious about him, he wore his heart on his sleeve. He was a tryer, he worked hard. He was one of the best contestants I've worked with."

(......................... on watching Olly in The X Factor)

5. "If you loved *Please Don't Let Me Go* then get your diapers ready ... it's so good you'll poop!"

(......................... on Olly's latest song)

A. OLLY'S MUM

B. CAROLINE FLACK

C. NICK RAPHAEL, HEAD OF EPIC RECORDS

D. EDDIE, LOVEABLE ROGUES

6. "We hope to have some time off in January. It would be such a laugh to go away with Olly. He is such a fun guy."
(........................ on Olly's holiday plans)

7. "I tried to team him up with one of my mates but I don't think it went very well! Olly will find the right girl, but he's so busy at the moment."
(........................ on Olly's love life)

8. "If you meet him, if you see him, people that work with him, they like him. It's very hard for us to find artists that people like."
(........................ on Olly's appeal)

TALK

THESE PAGES ARE BUBBLING OVER WITH OLLY CHATTER! READ THROUGH THE QUOTES AND THEN TRY TO DECIDE WHO IS TALKING ABOUT THE STAR EACH TIME. THE NAMES ARE LISTED IN RANDOM ORDER BELOW – TAKE YOUR PICK!

E. JORDAN, RIZZLE KICKS

F. CO-WRITER, CLAUDE KELLY

G. OLLY'S MANAGER, SARAH

H. SIMON COWELL

Awards & Nominations

Olly has proved himself to be an established musician and artist just take a look at the incredible list of nominations he's received over the past few years! Olly, despite losing out to Emeli Sandé, was especially delighted to be nominated for an Ivor Novello Award in 2013. The Ivors are hugely prestigious prizes given for song-writing and composing. Although bagging a BRIT Award has eluded Olly so far, we know it's only a matter of time before his trophy cabinet will be bursting at the hinges!

2013

Best Live Act,
Nordoff Robbins 02 Silver Clef
Awards
Nominated

British Male Solo Artist,
BRIT Awards
Nominated

Single of the Year for
Troublemaker,
BRIT Awards
Nominated

Best Crush Song for
Heart Skips A Beat,
Radio Disney Music Awards
Nominated

Best Acoustic Performance
for *Heart Skips A Beat,*
Radio Disney Music Awards
Nominated

Favourite UK Male Artist,
Nickelodeon's Kids Choice
Awards
Nominated

2012

Favourite UK Male Artist,
Nickelodeon's Kids Choice Awards
Winner

British Single for *Heart Skips A Beat*,
BRIT Awards
Nominated

PRS for Music Most Performed Work,
Ivor Novello Awards
Nominated

2011

Best Male Artist,
BT Digital Music Awards
Winner

Best British Album,
BBC Radio 1's Teen Awards
Winner

Best British Single for *Please Don't Let Me Go*,
BRIT Awards
Nominated

Best Newcomer Artist,
BT Digital Music Awards
Nominated

Olly gets ready to perform on **Good Morning America**.

Now that he's won the hearts and iPods of the UK market, it's only natural that Olly would set his sights on the holy grail of pop superstardom – the USA! After his tour of the states with One Direction in 2012, Olly has made great in-roads already. His last album hit the top five in the US iTunes charts and in May 2013 Olly celebrated selling 1.4 million copies of his smash single *Troublemaker*.

Now Mr Murs is described as a *'British Sensation'*! He performed a series of concerts during the Spring which saw the artist travelling to a host of North American cities. From Tampa to Toronto, everybody loved Olly!

Olly says advanced technology and social media has helped him become a hit across the pond, but we think it's just the Murs factor! He's already performed in Times Square for the massive TV show *Good Morning America* and strutted his stuff on *Dancing With The Stars*. After his cameo in *90210* and chart success, his future can only get bigger and better!

Rocking the Z100 and Coca-Cola All Access lounge.

Being interviewed on Y100 radio station, Miami.

© Lorenzo Bevilaqua/ABC via Getty Images

Appearing on *The View*.

BREAKING THE STATES

THE OFFICIAL OLLY QUIZ PART 3

This is it – the last part of Olly's super-fan challenge! These 15 quiz questions will sort the die-hards from the try-hards ... Grab a pencil, then put on your thinking cap. Anyone that can nail at least 10 correct answers deserves to be known as a true Olly aficionado. Good luck!

1. What is the name of Olly's favourite sweet?

2. Name the song that Olly performed onstage with Robbie during his massive 2013 stadium tour.

3. What office job was Olly doing when he auditioned for *The X Factor*?

4. Where did Olly shoot the video for *Dear Darlin'*?

5. When did Olly move out of his parents' house?

6. What talk show brought Olly face-to-face with his movie star crush, Mila Kunis?

7. When is Olly's birthday?

8. What is Olly's biggest hit to date in America?

9. The video to which single shows Olly turning up at a party a huge country house?

10. What embarrassing thing happened to Olly when he performed at *Guilfest 2012*?

11. Why did Olly decide to leave *The Xtra Factor* after two successful years??

12. Which hot boy band did Olly tour the US with in 2012?

13. Which quiz show has Olly appeared on twice, even though he's never won much cash?

14. How many UK number one singles has Olly had?

15. For which event did Olly represent the England in both 2010 and 2012?

OLLY'S SCRAPBOOK

When you live life at 100 miles per hour, you don't often get the chance to sit back and smell the roses. But no matter how crazy his schedule is, Olly never forgets the amazing things that have happened to him. Would you like to take a peek into Olly's scrapbook? Here are some of his favourite memories, collected especially for you ...

Feeling the love with fans Down Under.

Every artist dreams of seeing their name up in lights!

Olly and Mila Kunis at The Graham Norton Show

Duetting with Gary Barlow
for the Prince's Trust

Backstage at The Tonight
Show With Jay Leno

Wearing the England
shirt with pride!

Olly playing Fifa with
Wayne Rooney

The blast that was touring with One Direction

Olly performs on stage with Madness

Just another day's work at the O2 Arena!

Stealing a kiss from the divine Miss Piggy

Performing with JLS for
Sport Relief

A very patriotic number
for the BRIT Awards!

Olly in Toronto on the
One Direction tour

My favourite place
in the world ...

MR MURS

A is for *Army of Two*
The heartfelt anthem Olly dedicated to his fans.

B is for BRITS
Olly's only been nominated so far, but we know there's a statue with his name on it waiting in the wings!

C is for Caroline Flack
Olly's co-host on *The Xtra Factor*.

D is for *Dear Darlin'*
Olly's haunting ballad about a guy writing a letter to his ex.

E is for Essex
The place that Olly will always call home.

F F is for football
Olly's number one sport!

G is for *Good Morning America*
The massive TV show across the pond that Olly has performed on.

H is for hats
Olly's got a bit of a reputation for them

I is for Ivor Novello
The prestigious song-writing award that Olly was nominated for.

J is for JLS
Olly and the band always have a riot when they get together!

K is for Kaisut
The desert that Olly trekked across to raise money for Comic Relief

L is for *Loveable Rogues*
The *Britain's Got Talent* stars that supported Olly on his arena tour.

M is for Malia
The place that Olly to went for a lads' holiday after finding fame in *The X Factor*.

FROM A TO Z

N is for **Notley FC**
Olly's local footie team. He even still plays for them every now and again!

O is for **One Direction**
After months' touring the length and breadth of the USA, 1D and Olly are firm pals.

P is for **Please Don't Let Me Go**
The massive TV show across the pond that Olly has performed on.

Q is for **quiz**
When it comes to TV quizzes, Olly hasn't had much luck. Better not mention *Deal Or No Deal*!

R is for **Rizzle Kicks**
... but Olly's bud Robbie needs a mention, too!

S is for **Stanley**
Olly's middle name.

T is for **Troublemaker**
An all-round, epic song and the one that changed everything for Olly in the USA.

U is for **Unicef**
The charity Olly supported twice when he kitted up for Soccer Aid.

V is for **V Festival**
One of Olly's favourite dates on the festival circuit

W is for **'Wiggle'**
We all love it when Olly performs his bottom-shaking dance move!

X is for **X Factor**
How could it not?!

Y is for **You**
the magnificent Murs' army!

Z is for **Zzzzzz ...**
Olly grabs some of this when ever he can, he loves his shut eye!

DEAR DARLIN'

With his cheeky chappy image and upbeat pop tunes, Olly surprised everybody in May 2013 by releasing a soulful ballad. *Dear Darlin'* tells the story of a guy writing a letter to his ex, pouring his heart out about how much he misses her. It was a theme that Olly could relate to – he can remember writing letters to a girlfriend he once had in Leeds.

The single jumped straight into the iTunes top 10, capturing the hearts of thousands of fans. The official *Dear Darlin'* video features Olly in an empty apartment, thinking about how everything went wrong in his relationship. For the lyric video, Olly invited his fans to submit pictures of themselves holding up the words to the song. The result is intimate and touching – fitting the music perfectly.

Can you sing *Dear Darlin'* with your eyes closed? Let's find out! Look through the lyrics, writing in the missing words.

Dear Darlin', please excuse
my writing
I can't stop my hands from
....
'Cos I'm cold and alone tonight
I miss you and nothing
.... like no you
And no one understands what we
went through
It was short, it was sweet, we tried

And if my words break through
the ....
And meet you at your door
All I can say is girl I mean them all

Dear Darlin', please excuse
my ....
I can't stop my hands from shaking
'Cos I'm cold and alone tonight
I miss you and nothing hurts like
.... you
And no one understands what we
went through
It was short, it was ....,
we tried, we tried

Woman:
I understand why we split before
a month

Been thinking about the bar we
drank in
Feeling like the sofa was sinking
I was .... in the hold of
your eyes

So if my words break through
the wall
To meet you at your ....
All I can say is girl I mean them all

Dear Darlin', please excuse
my writing
I can't stop my hands from shaking
cause I'm .... and
alone tonight
I miss you and nothing hurts like
no you
And no one understands what
we went through
It was short, it was sweet,
we ....

Oh I can't cope
These .... are yours
to hold

I miss you and nothing hurts like
no you
And no one .... what we
went through
It was short, it was sweet and we
tried, and we tried

WHAT'S NEXT?

So where will we see Olly in 2014? There'll certainly be more gigs, hits and TV shows, but we bet there will be a few surprises too! Olly's career has already taken some amazing twists and turns – from scoring platinum records to rocking the stadiums of Europe alongside Robbie.

Things are always changing for Olly, but he takes it in his stride. Why? Because he knows he can count on one thing – his loyal fans. Olly credits all of his success to us, the peeps that love his music, sound and style!

Here's to a poptastic, Olly-tastic 2014.

Let's have it!

To all my fans.
With love,
Olly
xxxx

ANSWERS

PAGES 18-19 Olly Murs Crossword

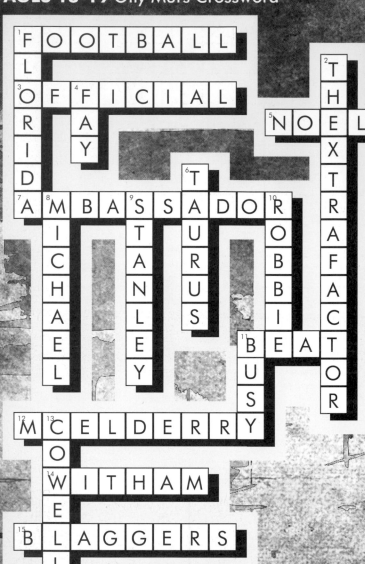

The crossword answers include:
FOOTBALL, FLORIDA, OFFICIAL, FAY, THE EXTRA FACTOR, NOEL, AMBASSADOR, MICHAEL, STANLEY, TAURUS, ROBBIE, BEAT, BUSY, MCELDERRY, MOWELL, WITHAM, BLAGGERS

PAGE 34
Mix It Up!

1. THINKING OF ME
2. BUSY
3. LOVE SHINE DOWN
4. ARMY OF TWO
5. ACCIDENTAL
6. HOLD ON
7. OH MY GOODNESS
8. DEAR DARLIN'

PAGES 38-39
Dance With Me Tonight

Gentlemen	baby	morning
Olly	dance	dark
minute	heavy	Break
fight	music	tonight

PAGES 54-55
The Official Olly Quiz – Part II

1. NEWCASTLE
2. DERMOT O'LEARY
3. JOE MCELDERRY
4. VICKI-LYNN POLLARD
5. LOUIE
6. LOS ANGELES
7. CHIDDY BANG
8. KEITH LEMON
9. ROBBIE WILLIAMS
10. MILA KUNIS
11. ALTON TOWERS
12. PEREZ HILTON
13. MICHAEL BUBLÉ
14. BARBADOS
15. GARY BARLOW

PAGES 56-57
Troublemaker

hooked	brain
lip	run
middle	back
good	insane
heart	November
poison	Troublemaker

PAGES 20-21 *Heart Skips A Beat*

beat	heart	home
record	hung	lady
dancing	repeat	winner
spin	hold	alone

PAGES 24-25
The Official Olly Quiz – Part I

1. a.	6. b.	11. a.
2. c.	7. a.	12. c.
3. c.	8. a.	13. a.
4. a.	9. b.	14. b.
5. b.	10. c.	15. b.

Hearsay And Headlines

1. True. During their stadium tour, kind Olly offered to look after Robbie's baby girl Teddy so he could have a romantic night out with his wife!
2. False. Olly just needs to warm up with a few vocal exercises.
3. True. Olly recently admitted that he'd love to go into acting, especially if he could emulate action movie stars like Sly Stallone or Jason Statham!
4. True. Olly's car got stuck in traffic on the way to the awards so he had to hop out at London Bridge and make a run for it!
5. True. Olly made a blistering start to 2013 when his single *Troublemaker* raced up the American singles charts.
6. True. Olly once lost control of his car when out driving on icy roads. The shunt injured his arm, but he made a speedy recovery.
7. False. Olly would never ignore his fans!
8. True. Olly made his fans giggle when he used an app to post a picture of himself on Twitter with geeky glasses and zits!
9. False. Olly would love a pet, but it's not practical when you're a globe-trotting pop star!
10. True. Olly openly admits that he can't get enough of being on stage.

Army of Two

walls	moment
love	future
swimming	hope
connection	change
bullet	hand
band	truth

O	L	J	E	V	A	R	E	N	A	P	G	M	A
L	W	A	Q	R	R	L	O	A	F	E	R	S	L
L	I	X	D	H	Y	P	P	A	H	X	Z	L	B
Y	T	F	S	O	V	F	M	A	T	E	S	S	U
O	H	L	E	S	M	A	N	A	G	E	R	H	M
F	A	T	U	O	S	D	J	Y	D	V	W	U	N
F	M	I	K	C	N	Q	N	B	C	X	F	O	K
I	T	Y	Z	C	T	M	K	L	Y	K	R	E	E
C	C	H	E	E	K	Y	U	I	M	U	Y	D	C
I	Q	J	L	R	H	H	B	R	O	Z	N	I	N
A	Z	E	W	A	G	A	C	T	S	P	I	V	A
L	L	B	G	I	G	T	M	Y	P	F	W	L	D
S	K	A	P	D	V	F	B	R	N	S	T	I	J
L	A	S	R	A	E	H	E	R	G	D	N	A	B

Olly Talk

1. G	4. H	7. B
2. D	5. F	8. C
3. A	6. E	

The Official Olly Quiz – Part III

1. Dip Dabs
2. *Kids*
3. He advised people on how to reduce their energy bills
4. Los Angeles
5. Only in 2012
6. *The Graham Norton Show*
7. 14th May
8. *Troublemaker*
9. *Please Don't Let Me Go.*
10. He slipped down a staircase at the side of the stage
11. To make more time for his music.
12. One Direction
13. *Deal Or No Deal*
14. Four
15. Soccer Aid

Dear Darlin'

shaking	no	cold
hurts	sweet	tried
wall	warm	arms
writing	door	understands